MEISTER ECKHART'S SERMONS

BY

JOHANNES ECKHART

AND

ON CLEAVING TO GOD

BY

ALBERT THE GREAT

MEISTER ECKHART'S SERMONS

JOHANNES ECKHART

TRANSLATED INTO ENGLISH BY

CLAUD FIELD

CONTENTS

PREFACE

"Meister Eckhart," who has been called the "Father of German thought," was a Dominican monk, and one of the most profound thinkers of the Middle Ages. He was born about 1260 A.D. in Thuringia, and died at Cologne 1327 A.D. In 1295 he was Prior of the Dominicans at Erfurt and Vicar-General of Thuringia. In 1300 he was sent to the University of Paris, where he studied Aristotle and the Platonists, and took the degree of Master of Arts. It is possible also that he taught at Paris. He already had a wide reputation as a philosopher, and was summoned to Rome in 1302 to assist Pope Boniface VIII. in his struggle against Philip the Fair. In 1304 he became Provincial of his order for Saxony, and in 1307 Vicar-General of Bohemia. In 1311 he was sent again to act as professor of theology in the school of Dominicans in Paris, and afterwards in Strasburg. Everywhere his teaching and preaching left a deep mark. At Strasburg he aroused suspicions and created enemies; his doctrine was accused of resembling that of the heretical sects of the "Beghards" and "Brothers of the Holy Spirit." The Superior-General of the Order had his writings submitted to a close examination by the Priors of Worms and Mayence. The history of this episode is very obscure. It appears that Eckhart was cited before the tribunal of the Inquisition at Cologne, and that he professed himself willing to withdraw anything that his writings might contain contrary to the teaching of the Church. The matter was referred to the Pope, who, in 1329, condemned certain propositions extracted from the writings of Eckhart two years after the death of the latter.

The importance of Eckhart in the history of scholastic philosophy is considerable. At that period all the efforts of religious philosophy were directed to widen theology, and to effect a reconciliation between reason and faith. The fundamental idea of Eckhart's philosophy is that of the Absolute or Abstract Unity conceived as the sole real existence. His God is the Theos agnostos of the neoplatonists: He is absolutely devoid of attributes which would be a limitation of His Infinity. God is incomprehensible; in fact, with regard to our limited intelligence, God is the origin and final end of every being. How then, it may be asked, can God be a Person? The answer is, that by the eternal generation of the Son the Father becomes conscious of Himself, and the Love reflected back to the Father by the Son is the Holy Spirit. Together with the Son, God also begets the ideal forms of created things. The Absolute is thus the common background of God and the Universe. Like as the Son does, so everything born of God tends to return to Him, and to lose itself in the unity of His Being.

This theology is really Pantheism. Of the Absolute we have no cognizance but only of phenomena, but by the resolute endeavour to abstract ourselves from time and space, we can, according to Eckhart, at rare moments, attain to the Absolute by virtue of what he calls "the spark" (Funkelein) of the soul, which comes direct from God. This is really God acting in man; to know God is to be one with God. This is the final end of all our activity, and the means of attaining thereto is complete quietism. But Eckhart shrank from carrying his doctrines out to their extreme logical conclusion, though some of the more fanatical among his followers did so. On account of his insistence on the immediacy of man's approach to God, apart from Church institutions, he may be justly regarded as a fore-runner of the Reformation.

Note.--The best account of Eckhart in English is probably to be found in Vaughan's "Hours with the Mystics," vol. i.

ECKHART'S SERMONS

I

THE ATTRACTIVE POWER OF GOD

St John vi. 44.--"No one can come unto Me, except the Father which hath sent Me draw him."

Our Lord Jesus Christ hath in the Gospel spoken with His own blessed lips these words, which signify, "No man can come to Me unless My Father draw him." In another place He says, "I am in the Father and the Father in Me." Therefore whoever cometh to the Son cometh to the Father. Further, He saith, "I and the Father are One. Therefore whomsoever the Father draweth, the Son draweth likewise." St Augustine also saith, "The works of the Holy Trinity are inseparable from each other." Therefore the Father draweth to the Son, and the Son draweth to the Holy Ghost, and the Holy Ghost draweth to the Father and the Son; and each Person of the Trinity, when He draweth to the Two Others, draweth to Himself, because the Three are One. The Father draweth with the might of His power, the Son draweth with His unfathomable wisdom, the Holy Ghost draweth with His love. Thus we are drawn by the Sacred Trinity with the cords of Power, Wisdom and Love, when we are drawn from an evil thing to a good thing, and from a good thing to a better, and from a better thing to the best of all. Now the Father draws us from the evil of sin to the goodness of His grace with the might of His measure-measureless power, and He needs all the resources of His strength in order to convert sinners, more than when He was about to make heaven and earth, which He made with His own power without help from any creature. But when He is about to convert a sinner, He always needs the sinner's help. "He converts thee not without thy help," as St Augustine says.

Therefore deadly sin is a breach of nature, a death of the soul, a disquiet of the heart, a weakening of power, a blindness of the sense, a sorrow of the spirit, a death of grace, a death of virtue, a death of good works, an aberration of the spirit, a fellowship with the devil, an expulsion of Christianity, a dungeon of hell, a banquet of hell, an eternity of hell. Therefore, if thou committest a deadly sin thou art guilty of all these and incurrest their consequences. Regarding the first point: Deadly sin is a breach of nature, for every man's nature is an image and likeness and mirror of the Trinity, of Godhead and of eternity. All these together are marred by a deadly sin; therefore, it is a breach of nature. Such sin is also the death of the soul, for death is to lose life. Now God is the life of the soul, and deadly sin separates from God; therefore it is a death of the soul. Deadly sin is also a disquiet of the heart, for everything rests nowhere except in its own proper place; and the proper resting-place of the soul is nowhere except in God as St Augustine saith, "Lord! Thou hast made us for Thyself, therefore we may not rest anywhere save in Thee." Deadly sin is also a weakening of the powers, for by his own power no one can throw off the load of sin nor restrain himself from committing sin. It is also a blindness of the sense, for it prevents a man recognizing how brief is the space of time that can be spent in the pleasure of voluptuousness, and how long are the pains of hell and the joys of heaven. Deadly sin is also a death of all grace, for whenever such a sin is committed, the soul is bereft of all grace. Similarly, it is the death of all virtue and good works, and an aberration of the spirit.

It is also a fellowship with the Devil, for everything hath fellowship with its like; and sin maketh the soul and Satan resemble each other. It is also an expulsion of Christianity, for it depriveth the sinner of all the profit that comes from Christianity. It is also a dungeon of hell, for if the soul remain in the purity in which God created her, neither angel nor devil may rob her of her freedom. But sin confines it in hell. Sin is also an eternity of hell, for eternity is in the will, and were it not in the will, it would not be in the consciousness.

Now, people say when they commit sin, that they do not intend to do so always; they intend to turn away from sin. That is just as though a man were to kill himself and suppose that he could make himself alive again by his own strength. That is, however, impossible; but to turn from sin by one's own power and come to God is still much more impossible. Therefore, whosoever is to turn from sin and come to God in His heavenly kingdom, must be drawn by the heavenly Father with the might of His divine power. The Father also draws the Son who comes to help us with His grace, by stimulating our free will to turn away from, and hate sin, which has drawn us aside from God, and from the immutable goodness of the Godhead. Then, if she is willing, He pours the gift of His grace into the soul, which renounces all her misery and sin, and all her works become living. Now, this grace springs from the centre of Godhead and the Father's heart, and flows perpetually, nor ever ceases, if the soul obeys His everlasting love. Therefore He saith in the prophets: "I have loved thee with an everlasting love, therefore with loving kindness have I drawn thee." Out of the overflow of His universal love He desires to draw all to Himself, and to His Only-begotten Son, and to the Holy Ghost in the joy of the heavenly kingdom. Now, we should know that before our Lord Jesus Christ was born, the Heavenly Father drew men with all His might for five thousand, two hundred years; and yet, as far as we know, brought not one into the heavenly kingdom. So, when the Son saw that the Father had thus strongly drawn men and even wearied Himself, and yet not succeeded, He said to the Father: "I will draw them with the cords of a man." It was as though He said, "I see well, Father, that Thou with all Thy might, canst not succeed, therefore will I myself draw them with the cords of a man."

Therefore the Son came down from heaven, and was incarnate of a Virgin, and took upon Him all our bodily weaknesses, except sin and folly, into which Adam had cast us; and out of all His words and works and limbs and nerves, He made a cord, and drew us so skillfully, and so heartily, that the bloody sweat poured from His sacred Body. And when He had drawn men without ceasing for three and thirty years, He saw the beginnings of a movement and the redemption of all things that would follow. Therefore He said, "And I, if I be lifted up on the Cross, will draw all men unto Me." Therefore He was stretched upon the Cross, and laid aside all His glory, and whatever might hinder His drawing men.

Now, there are three natural means of attraction with which Christ on the Cross drew to Himself between the third and the ninth hour, more people than He had drawn before during the three and thirty years of His life. The first means by which He draws is affinity, that affinity which brings creatures of the same species together, and like to its like. With this cord of affinity he drew men to the Godhead, Whom He always resembles. In order that God may draw more to Himself, and forget His wrath, the Son saith, "Beloved Father, seeing that Thou wouldest not forgive sins because of all the former sacrifices offered, lo I, Thine Only begotten Son, Who resemble Thy Godhead in all things, in Whom Thou hast hidden all the riches of divine love, I come to the Cross, that I may be a living sacrifice before Thine eyes; that out of Thy fatherly compassion Thou mayest bend and look on Me, Thine only Son, and on My Blood flowing from My wounds, and slake the fiery sword with which in the angel's hands Thou hast barred the way to Paradise, that all who have repented and bewailed their sins through Me, may enter therein."

The second means of attraction which He used is Emptiness, as we see when we place one end of a hollow pipe in water, and draw up it by suction; the water runs up the stem to the mouth, because the emptiness of the pipe, from which the air has been drawn, draws the water to itself. So

Our Lord Jesus Christ made Himself empty that He might wisely draw all things to Himself. Therefore He let all the blood that was in His Body flow out, and so attracted to Himself all the compassion and grace that was in His Father's heart, so completely and profitably as to suffice for the whole world. Accordingly, the Father said, "My compassion will I never forget," and further, "Now, My Son, be bold and strong that Thou mayest lead the people altogether into the land which I have promised, the land of heavenly joys, the land which floweth with the honey of My Godhead, and with the milk of Thy manhood."

The third means of attraction is this--that as we see the sun draw up the mists from the earth to heaven, so the heart of our Lord Jesus Christ waxed hot as a fiery furnace upon the Cross, so fiercely burned the flame of love which He felt towards the whole world. Thus, with the heat of His love, from which nothing could be hidden, so intense was it--He drew the whole world to Himself. Never did our Lord Jesus Christ display such great love as when He suffered the torture of the Cross when He gave His life for us, and washed our sins with His precious Blood. Therefore with the cords of Love, He drew us all to Himself upon the Cross that those who feel the drawing of His death and martyrdom might live with Him in everlasting felicity.

14

Now when the Holy Spirit saw that the Only Begotten Son of the Father had drawn so wisely that He had won to Himself all things in heaven and earth, He also felt impelled by His own love and kindness to draw. Therefore He said, "I will also draw with My cords and My net." So He made a net of the seven high attributes of the Father, of the seven graces of the Son, of His own seven gifts, and of the seven Christian virtues. Thus He assures us that we shall never perish, for we are so caught by His goodness that He expels from us all the evil works of the flesh, and produces in us His fruits, so that we gain the reward of everlasting life. May the Father of His love, and the Son of His grace, and the Holy Spirit with His fellowship, grant us to be worthy of the same. Amen.

II

THE NEARNESS OF THE KINGDOM

St Luke xxi. 31.--"Know that the Kingdom of God is near."

Our Lord saith that the Kingdom of God is
near us. Yea, the Kingdom of God is within us as
St Paul saith "our salvation is nearer than when we
believed." Now we should know in what manner
the Kingdom of God is near us. Therefore let us
pay diligent attention to the meaning of the words.
If I were a king, and did not know it, I should not
really be a king. But, if I were fully convinced that
I was a king, and all mankind coincided in my belief, and I knew that they shared my conviction, I
should indeed be a king, and all the wealth of the
king would be mine. But, if one of these three
conditions were lacking, I should not really be a
king.

In similar fashion our salvation depends upon
our knowing and recognizing the Chief Good
which is God Himself. I have a capacity in my
soul for taking in God entirely. I am as sure as I

live that nothing is so near to me as God. God is nearer to me than I am to myself; my existence depends on the nearness and presence of God. He is also near things of wood and stone, but they know it not. If a piece of wood became as aware of the nearness of God as an archangel is, the piece of wood would be as happy as an archangel. For this reason man is happier than the inanimate wood, because he knows and understands how God is near him. His happiness increases and diminishes in proportion to the increase and diminution in his knowledge of this. His happiness does not arise from this that God is near him, and in him, and that He possesses God; but from this, that he knows the nearness of God, and loves Him, and is aware that "the Kingdom of God is near." So, when I think on God's Kingdom, I am compelled to be silent because of its immensity, because God's Kingdom is none other than God Himself with all His riches. God's Kingdom is no small thing: we may survey in imagination all the worlds of God's creation, but they are not God's Kingdom. In whichever soul God's Kingdom appeareth, and which knoweth God's Kingdom, that soul needeth no human preaching or instruction; it is taught from within and assured of eternal life. Whoever knows and recognizes how near God's Kingdom is to him may say with Jacob, "God is in this place, and I knew it not."

God is equally near in all creatures. The wise man saith, ¨God hath spread out His net over all creatures, so that whosoever wishes to discover Him may find and recognize Him in each one.¨ Another saith, ¨He knows God rightly who recognizes Him alike in all things.¨ To serve God with fear is good; to serve Him out of love is better; but to fear and love Him together is best of all. To have a restful or peaceful life in God is good; to bear a life of pain in patience is better; but to have peace in the midst of pain is the best of all.

A man may go into the field and say his prayer and be aware of God, or, he may be in Church and be aware of God; but, if he is more aware of Him because he is in a quiet place, that is his own deficiency and not due to God, Who is alike present in all things and places, and is willing to give Himself everywhere so far as lies in Him. He knows God rightly who knows Him everywhere. St Bernard saith, ¨How is it that mine eye and not my foot sees heaven? Because mine eye is more like heaven than my foot is. So, if my soul is to know God, it must be God-like.¨

Now, how is the soul to arrive at this heavenly state that it recognizes God in itself, and knows that He is near? By copying the heavens, which can receive no impulse from without to mar their tranquility. Thus must the soul, which would know God, be rooted and grounded in Him so steadfastly, as to suffer no perturbation of fear or hope, or joy or sorrow, or love or hate, or anything which may disturb its peace.

The heavens are everywhere alike remote from earth, so should the soul be remote from all earthly things alike so as not to be nearer to one than another. It should keep the same attitude of aloofness in love and hate, in possession and renouncement, that is, it should be simultaneously dead, resigned and lifted up. The heavens are pure and clear without shadow of stain, out of space and out of time. Nothing corporeal is found there. Their revolutions are incredibly swift and independent of time, though time depends on them. Nothing hinders the soul so much in attaining to the knowledge of God as time and place. Therefore, if the soul is to know God, it must know Him outside time and place, since God is neither in this or that, but One and above them. If the soul is to see God, it must look at nothing in time; for while the soul is occupied with time or place or any image of the kind, it cannot recognize God. If it is to know Him, it must have no fellowship with nothingness. Only he knows God who recognizes that all creatures are nothingness. For, if one creature be set over against another, it may appear to be beautiful and somewhat, but if it be set over against God, it is nothing. I say moreover: If the soul is to know God it must forget itself and lose itself, for as long as it contemplates self, it cannot contemplate God. When it has lost itself and everything in God, it finds itself again in God when it attains to the knowledge of Him, and it finds also everything which it had abandoned complete in God. If I am to know the highest good, and the everlasting Godhead, truly, I must know them as they are in themselves apart from creation. If I am to know real existence, I must know it as it is in itself, not as it is parceled out in creatures.

The whole Being of God is contained in God alone. The whole of humanity is not contained in one man, for one man is not all men. But in God the soul knows all humanity, and all things at their highest level of existence, since it knows them in their essence. Suppose any one to be in a beautifully adorned house: he would know much more about it than one who had never entered therein, and yet wished to speak much about it. Thus, I am as sure, as I am of my own existence and God's, that, if the soul is to know God, it must know Him outside of time and place. Such a soul will know clearly how near God's kingdom is.

Schoolmen have often asked how it is possible for the soul to know God. It is not from severity that God demands much from men in order to obtain the knowledge of Himself: it is of His kindness that He wills the soul by effort to grow capacious of receiving much, and that He may give much. Let no man think that to attain this knowledge is too difficult, although it may sound so, and indeed the commencement of it, and the renouncement of all things, is difficult. But when one attains to it, no life is easier nor more pleasant nor more lovable, since God is always endeavouring to dwell with man, and teach him in order to bring him to Himself. No man desires anything so eagerly as God desires to bring men to the knowledge of Himself. God is always ready, but we are very unready. God is near us, but we are far from Him. God is within, and we are without. God is friendly; we are estranged. The prophet saith, "God leadeth the righteous by a narrow path into a broad and wide place, that is into the true freedom of those who have become one spirit with God." May God help us all to follow Him that He may bring us to Himself. Amen.

III

THE ANGEL'S GREETING

St Luke i. 28.--"Hail, thou that art highly favoured among women, the Lord is with thee."

Here there are three things to understand: the first, the modesty of the angel; the second, that he thought himself unworthy to accost the Mother of God; the third, that he not only addressed her, but the great multitude of souls who long after God.

I affirm that had the Virgin not first borne God spiritually He would never have been born from her in bodily fashion. A certain woman said to Christ, "Blessed is the womb that bear Thee." To which Christ answered, "Nay, rather blessed are they that hear the Word of God and keep it." It is more worthy of God that He be born spiritually of every pure and virgin soul, than that He be born of Mary. Hereby we should understand that humanity is, so to speak, the Son of God born from all eternity. The Father produced all creatures, and me among them, and I issued forth from Him with all creatures, and yet I abide in the Father. Just as the word which I now speak is conceived and spoken forth by me, and you all receive it, yet none the less it abides in me. Thus I and all creatures abide in the Father.

Hereto I adjoin a parable. There were a certain man and wife; the woman by accident lost an eye, and was sorely troubled thereat. Her husband then said to her, "Wife, why are you troubled?" She answered, "It is not the loss of my eye that troubles me, but the thought that you may love me less on account of that loss." He said, "I love you all the same." Not long after he put one of his own eyes out, and came to his wife and said, "Wife, that you may believe I love you, I have made myself like you: I, too, now, have only one eye." So men could hardly believe that God loved them till God put one of His eyes out, that is took upon Himself human nature, and was made man. Just as fire infuses its essence and clearness into the dry wood, so has God done with man. He has created the human soul and infused His glory into it, and yet in His own essence has remained unchangeable. If you ask me whether, seeing that my spiritual birth is out of time, whether I am an eternal son, I answer "Yes," and "No." In the everlasting foreknowledge of God, I slumbered like a word unspoken. He hath brought me forth His son in the image of His eternal fatherhood, that I also should be a father and bring forth Him.

It is as if one stood before a high mountain, and cried, "Art thou there?" The echo comes back, "Art thou there?" If one cries, "Come out." the echo answers, "Come out."

Again: If I am in a higher place and say to some one, "Come up hither," that might be difficult for him. But if I say, "Sit down," that would be easy. Thus God dealeth with us. When man humbles himself, God cannot restrain His mercy; He must come down and pour His grace into the humble man, and He gives Himself most of all, and all at once, to the least of all. It is essential to God to give, for His essence is His goodness and His goodness is His love. Love is the root of all joy and sorrow. Slavish fear of God is to be put away. The right fear is the fear of losing God. If the earth flee downward from heaven, it finds heaven beneath it; if it flee upward, it comes again to heaven. The earth cannot flee from heaven: whether it flee up or down, the heaven rains its influence upon it, and stamps its impress upon it, and makes it fruitful, whether it be willing or not. Thus doth God with men: whoever thinketh to escape Him, flies into His bosom, for every corner is open to Him. God brings forth His Son in thee, whether thou likest it or not, whether thou sleepest or wakest; God worketh His own will. That man is unaware of it, is man's fault, for his taste is so spoilt by feeding on earthly things that he cannot relish God's love. If we had love to God, we should relish God, and all His works; we should receive all things from God, and work the same works as He worketh.

God created the soul after the image of His highest perfection. He issued forth from the treasure-house of the everlasting Fatherhood in which He had rested from all eternity. Then the Son opened the tent of His everlasting glory and came forth from His high place to fetch His Bride, whom the Father had espoused to Him from all Eternity, back to that heaven from which she came. Therefore He came forth rejoicing as a bridegroom and suffered the pangs of love. Then He returned to His secret chamber in the silence and stillness of the everlasting Fatherhood. As He came forth from the Highest, so He returned to the Highest with His Bride, and revealed to her the hidden treasures of His Godhead.

The first beginning is for the sake of the last end. God Himself doth not rest because He is the beginning, but because He is the end and goal of all creation. This end is concealed in the darkness of the everlasting Godhead, and is unknown, and never was known, and never will be known. God Himself remains unknown; the light of the everlasting Father shineth in darkness, and the darkness comprehended it not. May the truth of which we have spoken lead us to the truth. Amen.

IV

TRUE HEARING

Ecclesiasticus xxiv. 30.—"Whoso heareth Me shall not be confounded."

The everlasting and paternal wisdom saith, "Whoso heareth Me is not ashamed." If he is ashamed of anything he is ashamed of being ashamed. Whoso worketh in Me sinneth not. Whoso confesseth Me and feareth Me, shall have eternal life. Whoso will hear the wisdom of the Father must dwell deep, and abide at home, and be at unity with himself. Three things hinder us from hearing the everlasting Word. The first is fleshliness, the second is distraction, the third is the illusion of time. If a man could get free of these, he would dwell in eternity, and in the spirit, and in solitude, and in the desert, and there would hear the everlasting Word. Our Lord saith, "No man can hear My word nor my teaching without renouncing himself." All that the Eternal Father teaches and reveals is His being, His nature, and

His Godhead, which He manifests to us in His Son, and teaches us that we are also His Son.

All that God worketh and teacheth, He worketh in His Son. All His work is directed to this end that we also may be His Son. When God sees that we are indeed His son, He yearns after us, and in the depth of His Divine Being waves of longing break forth, to reveal to us the abyss of His Godhead, and the fullness of His essence; He hastens to identify Himself with us. Herein He hath joy and gladness in full measure. God loveth men not less than He loveth Himself. If thou really lovest thyself, thou lovest all men as thyself; as long as thou lovest any one less than thyself, thou dost not really love thyself. That man is right who loves all men as himself.

Some folk say: "I love my friends, who do me kindness, more than other people." Such love is imperfect and incomplete; it is like having your sails only half-filled with wind. When I love anyone as much as myself, I would just as soon that joy or sorrow, death or life were mine, as well as his. That would be the dictate of right reason.

St Paul felt such love when he said, "I would that I were cut off from God for my friends' sake." Now to be cut off from God is equivalent to suffering the pains of hell. Some ask whether St Paul was on the way to perfection or was perfect. I answer, he was perfect, or he would have spoken otherwise.

I wish further to elucidate this saying of St Paul that he was willing to be cut off from God. The highest act of renunciation for man is for God's sake to give up God, and that is what St Paul was willing to do; to give up all the blessings that he might receive from God. When for God's sake he gave up God, God still remained with him, since God's essence is Himself, not any impression or reception of Himself. He who does so is a true man to whom no grief may happen, any more than it happens to the Divine Being. There is a somewhat in the soul that is, as it were, a blood-relative of God. It is one, it has nothing in common with nothing, nor is it like nothingness, nothing. All that is created is nothing, all far from and foreign to the soul. Could I but find myself one instant in that sphere of pure existence, I should regard myself as little as a worm.

A question arises regarding the angels who dwell with us, serve us and protect us, whether their joys are equal to those of the angels in heaven, or whether they are diminished by the fact that they protect and serve us. No, they are certainly not; for the work of the angels is the will of God, and the will of God is the work of the angels; their service to us does not hinder their joy nor their working. If God told an angel to go to a tree and pluck caterpillars off it, the angel would be quite ready to do so, and it would be his happiness, if it were the will of God.

The man who abides in the will of God wills nothing else than what God is, and what He wills. If he were ill he would not wish to be well. If he really abides in God's will, all pain is to him a joy, all complication, simple: yea, even the pains of hell would be a joy to him. He is free and gone out from himself, and from all that he receives, he must be free. If my eye is to discern colour, it must itself be free from all colour. The eye with which I see God is the same with which God sees me. My eye and God's eye is one eye, and one sight, and one knowledge, and one love.

The man who abides in God's love must be dead to himself and all created things, and regard himself as a mere unit among a thousand million. Such a man must renounce himself and all the world. Supposing a man possessed all the world, and gave it back to God intact just as he received it, God would give him back, all the world and everlasting life to boot. And supposing there were another man who had nothing but a good will, and he thought in his heart, "Lord, were all this world mine, and two worlds more beside it, I would give them and myself also back to Thee as I received them from thee"; to that man God would give back as much as he had given away. And supposing a man had renounced himself for twenty years, if he took himself back for a moment, that man's renunciation would be as nothing. The man who has truly renounced himself and does not once cast a glance on what he has renounced, and thus remains immovable and unalterable, that man alone has really renounced self. May God and the Eternal Wisdom grant us to remain equally immovable and unalterable with Himself. Amen.

V

THE SELF-COMMUNICATION OF GOD

St John xiv. 23.—"If a man love me, he will keep my words; and my Father will love him, and we will come unto him, and make our abode with him."

We read in the Gospels that Our Lord fed many people with five loaves and two fishes. Speaking parabolically, we may say that the first loaf was--that we should know ourselves, what we have been everlastingly to God, and what we now are to Him. The second--that we should pity our fellow Christian who is blinded; his loss should grieve us as much as our own. The third--that we should know our Lord Jesus Christ's life, and follow it to the utmost of our capacity. The fourth-- that we should know the judgments of God. All that may be said of the pains of hell is true. St Dionysius saith, "To be separated from God is hell, and the sight of God's countenance is heaven." The fifth is--that we should know the Godhead which has flowed into the Father and filled Him with joy, and which has flowed into the

Son and filled Him with wisdom, and the Two are essentially one. Therefore said Christ, "Where I am, there is My Father, and where My Father is, there am I" And They have flowed into the Holy Ghost and filled Him with good will. Therefore said Christ, "I and My Father have one Spirit," and the Holy Ghost has flowed into the soul.

The soul has by nature two capacities. The one is intelligence, which may comprehend the Holy Trinity with all its works and be contained by It as water is by a vessel. When the vessel is full, it has enclosed all that is contained in it, and is united with that which it has enclosed, and of which it is full. Thus intelligence becomes one with that which it has understood and comprehended. It is united therewith by grace, as the Son is one with the Father.

The second capacity is Will. That is a nobler one, and its essential characteristic is to plunge into the Unknown which is God. There the Will lays hold of God in a mysterious manner, and the Unknown God imparts His impress to the Will. The Will draws thought and all the powers of the soul after it in its train, so that the soul becomes one with God by grace, as the Holy Ghost is one with the Father and with the Son by nature. In God it is more worthy to be loved, than it is in itself. Therefore St Augustine saith that the soul is greater by its love-giving power than by its life-giving power. If man might only abide in this union, and do all the works which have ever been done by creatures, he would be no other than God, if his higher powers so brought his lower powers under control, that he could only work God-like works. That however may not be, and man's highest faculty therefore contemplates God as best it can, and so influences his lower faculties that they can discern between Good and Evil.

Adam possessed that union with God which we have spoken of, and while he had it, his capacity contained the capacities of all creatures. The load-stone attracts the needle, and the needle receives the magnetic power, so that it can also attract other needles and draw them to the load-stone. But if one draws the first needle away, all the other needles come with it. Thus was it with Adam: when, in his highest capacity, he was separated from God all his capacities deteriorated. Thence came also discord and the clashing of oppugnant wills among the lower creation, and deterioration of their powers down to the lowest. It is necessary, therefore, for all the creatures which issued forth from God to co-operate earnestly with all their powers to form a Man who may again attain that union with God which Adam enjoyed before he fell, and who may again restore to the creatures their forfeited powers. This is fulfilled in Christ as He Himself said, "I, if I be lifted up, will draw all men unto Me." He means, if He is exalted in our knowledge, He will draw us unto Himself. In Him human nature grew divine, and thanked God and loved Him with immeasurable love. This also befits God that he loves human nature with so great love. I counsel you, sisters and brothers, that you grow in knowledge, and thank God, while you are in time, that He brought you out of non-existence to existence, and united you with the Divine Nature. But if the Divine Nature be beyond your comprehension, believe simply on Christ; follow His holy example and remain steadfast. Convert Jews, heathen, heretics, bad Christians, and all who do not enjoy your knowledge of God, and are still astray.

Now rejoice, all ye powers of my soul, that you are so united with God that no one may separate you from Him. I cannot fully praise nor love Him therefore must I die, and cast myself into the divine void, till I rise from non-existence to existence. If I should remain entombed in flesh till the judgment day and suffer the pains of hell, that would be for me a small thing to bear for my beloved Lord Jesus Christ, if I had the certainty at last of not being separated from Him. While I am here, He is in me; after this life, I am in Him. All things are therefore possible to me, if I am united to Him Who can do all things. Previously I could not distinguish whether we were divine by nature or by grace. Then came Jesus and enlightened me so that I recognized in the Divine Nature Three

Persons, and that the Father was the Bringer-Forth of all things, as St James says, "every perfect gift cometh down from the Father of lights."

The Father and the Son have one Will, and that Will is the Holy Ghost, Who gives Himself to the soul so that the Divine Nature permeates the powers of the soul so that it can only do God-like works. Just as a spring, which perpetually flows and waters the roots of the flowers, so that the flowers bloom and receive their colours from the water of the spring, so the Godhead imparts Itself to the capacities of the soul that it may grow in the likeness of God. The more that the soul receives of the Divine Nature, the more it grows like It, and the closer becomes its union with God. It may arrive at such an intimate union that God at last draws it to Himself altogether, so that there is no distinction left, in the soul's consciousness, between itself and God, though God still regards it as a creature. Wherefore let yourselves not be misled by the light of nature. The higher the degree of knowledge which the soul attains to in the light of grace, the darker seems to it the light of nature. If the soul would know the real truth it must examine itself, whether it has withdrawn from all things, whether it has lost itself, whether it loves God purely with His love and nothing of its own at the same time, so that it may not be separated from Him by anything, and whether God alone dwells in it. If it has lost itself, it is as when the Virgin Mary lost Christ. She sought Him for three days, and yet was sure that she would find Him. All the while Christ was in the highest class in the school of His Father, unconscious of His mother's seeking Him. Thus happens it to the noble soul which goes to God to school, and learns there what God is in His essence, and what He is in the Trinity, and what He is in man, and what is most acceptable to Him. St Augustine saith that the righteousness of God in the Godhead and in the Trinity and in all creatures is the source of the chief joy which is in heaven. God in human nature is a lamp of living light, and "the light shineth in darkness and the darkness comprehendeth it not." The darkness must ever more flee the light, as the night flees day. Thus the soul learns to know God's will. St Paul saith, "This is God's will, our sanctification." And this is our sanctification, to know what we were before time; what we are in time, and what we shall be after time. Thus the soul loses itself in these three, and recketh naught of the body, till it comes to it in the temple, and obeys it without murmuring. The Father is a revelation of the Godhead, the Son is an image and countenance of the Father, and the Holy Ghost is an effulgence of that countenance, and a mutual love between Them, and these properties They have always possessed in Themselves. The Three Persons have stooped out of pity down to human nature, and the Son became man, and was the most despised man on the earth, and suffered pain at the hands of the creatures whom He Himself created with the Father, through Whose will He became man. Thus was Christ till His death, and when He rose from the dead then was seen the most despised of all men united with the Godhead in the Person of Christ.

VI

SANCTIFICATION [1]

St Luke x. 42.--"One thing is needful."

I have read many writings both of heathen philosophers and inspired prophets, ancient and modern, and have sought earnestly to discover what is the best and highest quality whereby man may approach most nearly to union with God, and whereby he may most resemble the ideal of himself which existed in God, before God created men. And after having thoroughly searched these writings as far as my reason may penetrate, I find no higher quality than sanctification or separation from all creatures. Therefore said our Lord to Martha, "One thing is necessary," as if to say, "whoso wishes to be untroubled and content, must have one thing, that is sanctification."

Various teachers have praised love greatly, as St Paul does, when he saith, "to whatever height I may attain, if I have not love, I am nothing." But I set sanctification even above love; in the first place because the best thing in love is that it compels me to love God. Now it is a greater thing that I compel God to come to me, than that I compel myself to go to God. Sanctification compels God to come to me, and I prove this as follows:--

Everything settles in its own appropriate place; now God's proper place is that of oneness and holiness; these come from sanctification; therefore God must of necessity give Himself to a sanctified heart.

In the second place I set sanctification above love, because love compels me to suffer all things for the sake of God; sanctification compels me to be the recipient of nothing but God; now, it is a higher state to be the recipient of nothing but God than to suffer all things for God, because in suffering one must have some regard to the person who inflicts the suffering, but sanctification is independent of all creatures.

Many teachers also praise humility as a virtue. But I set sanctification above humility for the following reason. Although humility may exist without sanctification, perfect sanctification cannot exist without perfect humility. Perfect humility tends to the annihilation of self; sanctification also is so close to self-annihilation that nothing can come between them. Therefore perfect sanctification cannot exist without humility, and to have both of these virtues is better than to have only one of them.

The second reason why I set sanctification above humility is that humility stoops to be under all creatures, and in doing so goes out of itself. But sanctification remains self-contained. But to remain contained within oneself is nobler than to go out of oneself for any purpose whatever; therefore saith the Psalmist, "The King's daughter is all glorious within," that is, all her glory is from her inwardness. Perfect sanctification has no inclination nor going-out towards any creature; it wishes neither to be above or below, neither to be like nor unlike any creature, but only to be one. Whosoever wishes to be this or that wishes to be somewhat; but sanctification wishes to be nothing.

But some one may say: "All virtues must have existed in fullness in Our Lady, therefore perfect sanctification must have been in her. If sanctification is higher than humility, why did Our Lady speak of her humility, and not of her sanctification, when she said, "For He hath regarded the lowliness of His handmaiden?" To this I answer that God possesses both sanctification and humility, so far as we may attribute virtues to God. Now thou shouldest know that His humility brought God to stoop down to human nature, and our Lady knew that He wished for the same quality in her, and in that matter had regard to her humility alone. Therefore she made mention of her humility and not of her sanctification, in which she re-remained unmoved and unaffected. If she had said, "He hath regarded the sanctification of His handmaiden," her sanctification would have been disturbed, for, so to speak, would have been a going out of herself. Therefore the Psalmist said, "I will hear what the Lord God will say in me," as if to say, "If God will Speak to me, let Him come in, for I will not come out." And Boethius saith, "Men, why seek ye outside you what is inside you--salvation?"

I set also sanctification above pity, for pity is only going out of oneself to sympathize with one's fellow-creature's sorrows. From such an out-going sanctification is free and abides in itself, and does not let itself be troubled. To speak briefly: when I consider all the virtues I find none so entirely without flaw and so conducive to union with God as sanctification.

The philosopher Avicenna says, "The spirit which is truly sanctified attains to so lofty a degree that all which it sees is real, all which it desires is granted, and in all which it commands, it is obeyed." When the free spirit is stablished in true sanctification, it draws God to itself, and were it placed beyond the reach of contingencies, it would assume the properties of God. But God cannot part with those to anyone; all that He can do for the sanctified spirit is to impart Himself to it. The man who is wholly sanctified is so drawn towards the Eternal, that no transitory thing may move him, no corporeal thing affect him, no earthly thing attract him. This was the meaning of St Paul when he said, "I live; yet not I; Christ liveth in me."

Now the question arises what is sanctification, since it has so lofty a rank. Thou shouldest know that real sanctification consists in this that the spirit remain as immovable and unaffected by all impact of love or hate, joy or sorrow, honour or shame, as a huge mountain is unstirred by a gentle breeze. This immovable sanctification causes man to attain the nearest likeness to God that he is capable of. God's very essence consists of His immovable sanctity; thence springs His glory and unity and impassibility. If a man is to become as like God as a creature may, that must be by sanctification. It is this which draws men upward to glory, and from glory to unity, and from unity to impassibility, and effects a resemblance between God and men. The chief agent in this is grace, because grace draws men from the transitory and purifies them from the earthly. And thou shouldest know that to be empty of all creature's love is to be full of God, and to be full of creature-love is to be empty of God.

God has remained from everlasting in immovable sanctity, and still remains so. When He created heaven and earth and all creatures, His sanctity was as little affected thereby as though He had created nothing. I say further: God's sanctity is as little affected by men's good works and prayers, as though they had accomplished none, and He is by those means no more favourably inclined towards men than if they ceased praying and working. I say even more: when the Divine Son became man and suffered, that affected the sanctity of God as little as though He had never become man at all.

Here some one may make the objection: "Are then all good works and prayers thrown away, since God is unmoved by them, and at the same time we are told to pray to Him for everything?" In answer to this I say that God from all eternity saw everything that would happen, and also when, and how He would make all creatures: He foresaw also all the prayers which would be offered, and which of them He would hear: He saw the earnest prayers which thou wilt offer tomorrow, but He will not listen to them tomorrow, because He heard them in eternity, before thou wast a man at all. If, however, thy prayer is half-hearted and not in earnest, God will not deny it now, seeing that He has denied it in eternity. Thus God remains always in His immovable sanctity, but sincere prayer and good works are not lost, for whoso doeth well, will be well rewarded.

When God appears to be angry or to do us a kindness, it is we who are altered, while He remains unchangeable, as the same sunshine is injurious to weak eyes and beneficial to strong ones, remaining in itself the same. Regarding this Isidorus in his book concerning the highest good says, "People ask what was God doing before He created heaven and earth, or whence came the new desire in God to create?" To this he answers, "No new desire arose in God, seeing that creation was everlastingly present in Him, and in His intelligence." Moses said to God, "When Pharaoh asks me who Thou art, what shall I answer?" God said, "Say, I AM hath sent me unto you," that is to say, "He Who is unchangeable hath sent me."

Perhaps some one may ask, "Was Christ then also unchangeable, when He said, My soul is troubled even unto death,' or Mary when she stood under the Cross and lamented?" Here, thou shouldest know that in every man are two kinds of men, the outer and the inner man. Every man, who loves God, only uses his outer senses so far as is absolutely necessary; he takes care that they do not drag him down to the level of the beasts, as they do some who might rather he termed beasts than men. The soul of the spiritual man whom God moves to love Him with all his powers concentrates all its forces on the inner man. Therefore He saith, "Thou shalt love the Lord thy God with all thy heart." Now, there are some who waste the powers of the soul for the use of the outer man; these are they who turn all their thoughts and desires towards transitory things, and know nothing of the inner life. But a good man sometimes deprives his outer man of all power that it may have a higher object, while sensualists deprive the inner man of all power to use it for the outer man.

The outer man may go through various experiences, while the inner man is quite free and immovable. Now both in Christ and in Our Lady there was an inner and an outer man; when they spoke of outward things, they did so with the outward man, while the inner man remained immovable.

It may be asked: "What is the object of this immovable sanctity?" I answer, "Nothing": that is, so far as God has His way with a man, for He has not His way with all men.

Although God is Almighty, He can only work in a heart when He finds readiness or makes it. He works differently in men than in stones. For this we may take the following illustration: if we bake in one oven three loaves of barley-bread, of rye-bread, and of wheat, we shall find the same heat of the oven affects them differently; when one is well-baked, another will be still raw, and another yet more raw. That is not due to the heat, but to the variety of the materials. Similarly God works in all hearts not alike but in proportion as He finds them prepared and susceptible. If the heart is to be ready for the highest, it must he vacant of all other things. If I wish to write on a white tablet, whatever else is written on the tablet, however noble its purport, is a hindrance to me. If I am to write, I must wipe the tablet clean of everything, and the tablet is most suitable for my purpose when it is blank. Similarly, if God is to write on my heart, everything else must come out of it till it is really sanctified. Only so can God work His highest will, and so the sanctified heart has no outward object at all.

The question arises: But what then does the sanctified heart pray for? I answer that when truly sanctified, it prays for nothing, for whosoever prays asks God to give him some good, or to take some evil from him. But the sanctified heart desires nothing, and contains nothing that it wishes to be freed from. Therefore it is free of all want except that it wants to be like God. St Dionysius commenting on the text, "Know ye not that all run, but one receiveth the prize?" says "this running is nothing else than a turning away from all creatures and being united to the Uncreated." When the soul gets to this point, it loses its own distinctiveness, and vanishes in God as the crimson of sunrise disappears in the sun. To this goal only pure sanctification can arrive.

St Augustine says. "the strong attraction of the soul to the Divine reduces everything to nothingness: on earth this attraction is manifested as sanctification. When this process has reached its culminating point, knowledge becomes ignorance, desire indifference and light darkness. The reason why God desires a sanctified heart more than any other is apparent when we ask the question, "What does God seek in all things?" The mouth of Wisdom says to us, "In all things I seek rest," and rest is to be found only in the sanctified heart; therein therefore God is more glad to dwell than in any other thing.

Thou shouldest also know that the more a man sets himself to be receptive of divine influence, the happier he is: who most sets himself so, is the happiest. Now no man can reach this condition of receptivity except by conformity with God, which comes from submission to God. This is what Saint Paul means when he says, "Put on the Lord Jesus Christ," that is "be conformed to Christ." Whosoever wishes to comprehend the lofty rank and benefit of sanctification must mark Christ's words to His disciples regarding His humanity, "It is profitable for you, that I go away, for, if I go not away, the Comforter will not come to you." As if to say, "Ye have so much desire towards my natural outward form, that ye cannot fully desire the Holy Spirit." Therefore put away forms and unite yourselves with formless Being, for God's spiritual comfort is only offered to those who despise earthly comfort.

Now, all thoughtful folk, mark me! no one can be truly happy, except he who abides in the strictest sanctification. No bodily and fleshly delight can ever take place with out spiritual loss, for the flesh lusteth against the spirit, and the spirit against the flesh. Therefore, the more a man fleeth from the created, the more the Creator hastens to him. And consider this: if the pleasure we take in the outward image of our Lord Jesus Christ diminishes our capacity for receiving the Holy Spirit, how much more must our unbridled desire for earthly comforts diminish it!

Therefore sanctification is the best of all things, for it cleanses the soul, and illuminates the conscience, and kindles the heart, and wakens the spirit, and girds up the loins, and glorifies virtue and separates us from creatures, and unites us with God. The quickest means to bring us to perfection is suffering; none enjoy everlasting blessedness more than those who share with Christ the bitterest pangs. Nothing is sharper than suffering, nothing is sweeter than to have suffered. The surest foundation in which this perfection may rest is humility; whatever here crawls in the deepest abjectness, that the Spirit lifts to the very heights of God, for love brings suffering and suffering brings love. Ways of living are many; one lives thus, and another thus; but whosoever will reach the highest life, let him in a few words hear the conclusion of the whole matter: keep thyself clear of all men, keep thyself from all imaginations that crowd upon the mind, free thyself from all that is contingent, entangling, and cumbersome and direct thy mind always to gazing upon God in thy heart with a steadfast look that never wavers: as for other spiritual exercises--fasting, watching and prayer-- direct them all to this one end, and practice them so far as they may be helpful thereto, so wilt thou win to perfection. Here some one may ask, "Who can thus gaze always without wavering at a divine object?" I answer: "No one who now lives." This has only been said to thee that thou mightest know what the highest is, and that thou mightest have desires after it. But when thou losest sight of the Divine, thou shouldest feel as if bereft of thine eternal salvation, and shouldest long to recover it, and watch over thyself at all times, and direct thy aims and longing towards it. May God be blessed for ever. Amen.

¹ That is separation from all outward things.

VII

OUTWARD AND INWARD MORALITY

I Cor. xv. 10.--"The Grace of God."

Grace is from God, and works in the depth of the soul whose powers it employs. It is a light which issues forth to do service under the guidance of the Spirit. The Divine Light permeates the soul, and lifts it above the turmoil of temporal things to rest in God. The soul cannot progress except with the light which God has given it as a nuptial gift; love works the likeness of God into the soul. The peace, freedom and blessedness of all souls consist in their abiding in God's will. Towards this union with God for which it is created the soul strives perpetually. Fire converts wood into its own likeness, and the stronger the wind blows, the greater grows the fire. Now by the fire understand love, and by the wind the Holy Spirit. The stronger the influence of the Holy Spirit, the brighter grows the fire of love; but not all at once, rather gradually as the soul grows. Light causes flowers and plants to grow and bear fruit; in animals it produces life, but in men blessedness. This comes from the grace of God, Who uplifts the soul, for if the soul is to grow God-like it must be lifted above itself.

To produce real moral freedom, God's grace and man's will must co-operate. As God is the Prime Mover of nature, so also He creates free impulses towards Himself and to all good things. Grace renders the will free that it may do everything with God's help, working with grace as with an instrument which belongs to it. So the will arrives at freedom through love, nay, becomes itself love, for love unites with God. All true morality, inward and outward, is comprehended in love, for love is the foundation of all the commandments.

All outward morality must be built upon this basis, not on self-interest. As long as man loves something else than God, or outside God, he is not free, because he has not love. Therefore there is no inner freedom which does not manifest itself in works of love. True freedom is the government of nature in and outside man through God; freedom is essential existence unaffected by creatures. But love often begins with fear; fear is the approach to love: fear is like the awl which draws the shoe-maker's thread through the leather.

As for outward works they are ordained for this purpose that the outward man may be directed to God. But the inner work, the work of God in the soul is the chief matter; when a man finds this within himself, he can let go externals. No law is given to the righteous, because he fulfils the law inwardly, and bears it in himself, for the least thing done by God is better than all the work of creatures. But this is intended for those who are enlightened by God and the Holy Scriptures.

But here on earth man never attains to being unaffected by external things. There never was a Saint so great as to be immovable. I can never arrive at a state when discord shall be as pleasing to my ears as harmony. Some people wish to do without good works. I say, "This cannot be." As soon as the disciples received the Holy Ghost, they began to work. When Mary sat at the feet of our Lord that was her school time. But afterwards when Christ went to heaven, and she received the Holy Spirit, she began to serve and was a handmaid of the disciples. When saints become saints, they begin to work, and so gather to the refuge of everlasting safety.

How can a man abide in love, when he does not keep God's commands which issue forth from love? How can the inner man be born in God, when the outer man abides not in the following of Christ, in self-mortification and in suffering, for

MEISTER ECKHART'S SERMONS

there is no being born of God, except through Christ. Love is the fulfilling of all commands; therefore however much man strives to reach this freedom, the body can never quite attain thereto, and must be ever in conflict. Seeing that good works are the witness of the Holy Ghost, man can never do without them. The aim of man is not outward holiness by works, but life in God, yet this last expresses itself in works of love.

Outward as well as inward morality helps to form the idea of true Christian freedom. We are right to lay stress on inwardness, but in this world there is no inwardness without an outward expression. If we regard the soul as the formative principle of the body, and God as the formative principle of the soul, we have a profounder principle of ethics than is found in Pantheism. The fundamental thought of this system is the real distinction between God and the world, together with their real inseparability, for only really distinct elements can interpenetrate each other.

The inner work is first of all the work of God's grace in the depth of the soul which subsequently distributes itself among the faculties of the soul, in that of Reason appearing as Belief, in that of Will as Love, and in that of Desire as Hope. When the Divine Light penetrates the soul, it is united with God as light with light. This is the

light of faith. Faith bears the soul to heights un-
reachable by her natural senses and faculties.

As the peculiar faculty of the eye is to see
form and colour, and of the ear to hear sweet tones
and voices, so is aspiration peculiar to the soul. To
relax from ceaseless aspiration is sin. This energy
of aspiration directed to and grasping God, as far
as is possible for the creature, is called Hope,
which is also a divine virtue. Through this faculty
the soul acquires such great confidence that she
deems nothing in the Divine Nature beyond her
reach.

The third faculty is the inward Will, which,
always turned to God like a face, absorbs to itself
love from God. According to the diverse directions in which redemptive Grace through the Holy
Spirit is imparted to the different faculties of men,
it finds corresponding expression as one of the
Spirit's seven gifts. This impartation constitutes
man's spiritual birth which brings him out of sin
into a state of grace while natural birth makes him
a sinner.

As God can only be seen by His own light, so
He can only be loved by His own love. The merely natural man is incapable of this, because nature
by itself is incapable of responding to the Divine
Love and is confined within its own circle. Therefore it is necessary for Grace, which is a simple

supernatural power, to elevate the natural faculties to union in God above the merely temporal objects of existence. The possibility of love to God is grounded in the relative likeness between man and God. If the soul is to reach its moral goal, i.e. Godlikeness, it must become inwardly like God through grace, and a spiritual birth which is the spring of true morality. The inner work that man has to do is the practical realization of Grace: without this, all outward work is ineffectual for salvation. Virtue is never mere virtue, it is either from God, or through God, or in God. All the soul's works which are to inherit an everlasting recompense must be carried on in God. They are rewarded by Him in proportion as they are carried on in Him, for the soul is an instrument of God whereby He carries on His work.

The essence of morality is inwardness, the intensity of will from which it springs, and the nobleness of the aim for which it is practiced. When a good work is done by a man, he is free of it, and through that freedom is liker and nearer to his Original than he was before.

The moral task of man is a process of spiritualization. All creatures are go-betweens, and we are placed in time that by diligence in spiritual business we may grow liker and nearer to God. The aim of man is beyond the temporal--in the serene region of the everlasting Present.

In this sense the New Birth of man is the focus towards which all creation strives, because man is the image of God after the likeness of which the world is created. All time strives towards eternity or the timeless Now, out of which it issued at creation. The merely temporal life in itself is a negation of real being, because it depends on itself and not on the deepest foundation of life; therefore also natural love is cramped finite and defective. It must through grace be lifted to the highest sphere of existence, and attain to freedom outside the narrow confines of the natural. Thereby love becomes real love, because only that is real which is comprehended and loved in its essence. Only by grace man comes from the temporal and transitory to be one with God. This lifting of manifoldness to unity is the supreme aim of ethics; by thus the divine birth is completed on the side of man.

This passage from nothingness to real being, this quitting of oneself is a birth accompanied by pain, for by it natural love is excluded. All grief except grief for sin comes from love of the world. In God is neither sorrow, nor grief, nor trouble. Wouldst thou be free from all grief and trouble, abide and walk in God, and to God alone. As long as love of the creature is in us, pain cannot cease.

This is the chief significance of the suffering of Christ for us, that we cast all our grief into the ocean of His suffering. If thou sufferest only regarding thyself, from whatever cause it may be, that suffering causes grief to thee, and is hard to bear. But if thou sufferest regarding God and Him alone, that suffering is not grievous, nor hard to bear, because God bears the load. The love of the Cross must swallow up our personal grief. Whoso does not suffer from love, for him sorrow is sorrow and grievous to bear; but whoso suffers from love he sorrows not, and his suffering is fruitful in God. Therefore is sorrow so noble; he who sorrows most is the noblest. Now no mortal's sorrow was like the sorrow which Christ bore; therefore he is far nobler than any man. Verily were there anything nobler than sorrow, God would have redeemed man thereby. Sorrow is the root of all virtue.

Through the higher love the whole life of man is to be elevated from temporal selfishness to the spring of all love, to God: man will again be master over nature by abiding in God and lifting her up to God.

ON CLEAVING TO GOD

ALBERT THE GREAT

CONTENTS

TRANSLATOR'S INTRODUCTION

This famous and much loved little treatise, On Cleaving to God, (De Adhaerendo Deo) has always been attributed to Saint Albert the Great, who lived from about 1200 to 1280, and was one of the most respected theologians of his time. He was moreover a voluminous writer in the scholastic tradition, and, amongst other things, Bishop of Ratisbonne and one of the teachers of Eckhart at Paris University. The Latin text of which this is a translation is found in volume 37 of his Opera Omnia published in Paris in 1898.

However almost all modern scholars are agreed that the work could not have been written by him, at least certainly not in its present form. It contains many implicit references and quotations from writers who lived well after Albert the Great. It is quite clear from the opening words of the treatise that it is in essence the private anthology of a contemplative or would-be contemplative, culled from many different sources, and including thoughts of his own. From the references included, it would seem to belong, at least in its present form to an unknown writer of the fifteenth century.

However, it has often been pointed out that the first nine chapters seem to be of a somewhat different character to the remaining seven. Indeed most of the directly contemplative and mystical material in the work is contained in this first half, while the second section is concerned largely with more general matters of ordinary Christian piety. It has therefore been suggested that it is perhaps possible that a later hand has to some extent reworked and extended an original, shorter text, that could perhaps even go back to Albert the Great. Albert, we know, wrote a commentary on the teachings of the famous St. Dionysius, and this work, particularly in the first nine chapters is full of "Dionysian" themes. This could indicate that these chapters at least may belong to Albert the Great, or, alternatively, it could explain how it came to be attributed to him. The fact remains, whichever way round, that the work stands on its own merits as a classic of Western contemplative mysticism in the Via Negativa tradition. It has indeed been frequently called a supplement to the Imitation of Christ.

In view of all these considerations, and in view of the fact that the work has always been attributed to Albert the Great (and all libraries and catalogues include it under his name), I have felt it best to leave it attached to his name, though with the above reservations. After all, Anonymous has dozens of works attributed to him that were actually written by someone else, so perhaps for once it is only fair to attribute an anonymous work to an actual person. Anyone who has ever tried to look for a work by Anonymous in a big library catalogue will, I feel confident, be grateful to me!

Like Anonymous, I lay no claims to copyright on this translation. I commit it, and a copy of the Latin original, to the deep in sure and certain hope that it will do its own work.

John Richards

CHAPTER 1

**On the highest and supreme perfection of man, in so far as it
is possible in this life**

I have had the idea of writing something for
myself on and about the state of complete and full
abstraction from everything and of cleaving
freely, confidently, nakedly and firmly to God
alone, so as to describe it fully (in so far as it is
possible in this abode of exile and pilgrimage),
especially since the goal of Christian perfection is
the love by which we cleave to God. In fact everyone is obligated, to this loving cleaving to God
as necessary for salvation, in the form of observ-
ing the commandments and conforming to the
divine will, and the observation of the commandments excludes everything that is contrary to the
nature and habit of love, including mortal sin.
Members of religious orders have committed
themselves in addition to evangelical perfection,
and to the things that constitute a voluntary and
counselled perfection by means of which one may
arrive more quickly to the supreme goal which is

God. The observation of these additional commitments excludes as well the things that hinder the working and fervour of love, and without which one can come to God, and these include the renunciation of all things, of both body and mind, exactly as one's vow of profession entails. Since indeed the Lord God is Spirit, and those who worship him must worship in spirit and in truth, in other words, by knowledge and love, that is, understanding and desire, stripped of all images. This is what is referred to in Matthew 6.6, When you pray, enter into your inner chamber,' that is, your inner heart, and having closed the door,' that is of your senses, and there with a pure heart and a clear conscience, and with faith unfeigned, pray to your Father,' in spirit and in truth, in secret.' This can be done best when a man is disengaged and removed from everything else, and completely recollected within himself. There, in the presence of Jesus Christ, with everything, in general and individually, excluded and wiped out, the mind alone turns in security confidently to the Lord its God with its desire. In this way it pours itself forth into him in full sincerity with its whole heart and the yearning of its love, in the most inward part of all its faculties, and is plunged, enlarged, set on fire and dissolved into him.

CHAPTER 2

How one can cling to and seek Christ alone, disdaining everything else

Certainly, anyone who desires and aims to arrive at and remain in such a state must needs above all have eyes and senses closed and not be inwardly involved or worried about anything, nor concerned or occupied with anything, but should completely reject all such things as irrelevant, harmful and dangerous. Then he should withdraw himself totally within himself and not pay any attention to any object entering the mind except Jesus Christ, the wounded one, alone, and so he should turn his attention with care and determination through him into him - that is, through the man into God, through the wounds of his humanity into the inmost reality of his divinity. Here he can commit himself and all that he has, individually and as a whole, promptly, securely and without discussion, to God's unwearying providence, in accordance with the words of Peter, cast all your care upon him (1 Peter 5.7), who can do everything. And again, In nothing be anxious (Philippians 4.6), or what is more, Cast your burden upon the Lord, and he will sustain you. (Psalm 55.22) Or again, It is good for me to hold fast to God, (Ps. 73.28) and I have always set up God before me. (Psalm 16.8) The bride too in the Song of Songs says, I have found him whom my soul loves, (Canticle 3.4) and again, All good things came to me along with her. (Wisdom 7.11) This, after all, is the hidden heavenly treasure, none other than the pearl of great price, which must be sought with resolution, esteeming it in humble faithfulness, eager diligence, and calm silence before all things, and preferring it even above physical comfort, or honour and renown. For what good does it do a religious if he gains the whole world but suffers the loss of his soul? Or what is the benefit of his state of life, the holiness of his profession, the virtue of his habit and tonsure, or the outer circumstances of his way of life if he is without a life of spiritual humility and truth in which Christ abides through a faith created by love. This is what Luke means by, the Kingdom of God (that is, Jesus Christ) is within you. (Luke 17.21)

CHAPTER 3

What the perfection of man consist of in this life

Now the more the mind is concerned about thinking and dealing with what is merely lower and human, the more it is separated from the experience in the intimacy of devotion of what is higher and heavenly, while the more fervently the memory, desire and intellect is withdrawn from what is below to what is above, the more perfect will be our prayer, and the purer our contemplation, since the two directions of our interest cannot both be perfect at the same time, being as different as light and darkness. He who cleaves to God is indeed translated into the light, while he who clings to the world is in the dark. So the supreme perfection of man in this life is to be so united to God that all his soul with all its faculties and powers are so gathered into the Lord God that he becomes one spirit with him, and remembers nothing except God, is aware of and recognises nothing but God, but with all his desires unified by the joy of love, he rests contentedly in the enjoyment of his Maker alone. Now the image of God as found in the soul consists of these three faculties, namely reason, memory and will, and so long as they are not completely stamped with God, the soul is not yet deiform in accordance with the initial creation of the soul. For the true pattern of the soul is God, with whom it must be imprinted, like wax with a seal, and carry the mark of his impress. But this can never be complete until the intellect is perfectly illuminated, according to its capacity, with the knowledge of God, who is perfect truth, until the will is perfectly focused on the love of the perfect good, and until the memory is fully absorbed in turning to and enjoying eternal happiness, and in gladly and contentedly resting in it. And since the glory of the beatitude which is achieved in our heavenly homeland consists in the complete fulfilment of these three faculties, it follows that perfect initiation of them is perfection in this life.

CHAPTER 4

How man's activity should be purely in the intellect and not in the senses

Happy therefore is the person who by continual removal of fantasies and images, by turning within, and raising the mind to God, finally manages to dispense with the products of the imagination, and by so doing works within, nakedly and simply, and with a pure understanding and will, on the the simplest of all objects, God. So eliminate from your mind all fantasies, objects, images and shapes of all things other than God, so that, with just naked understanding, intent and will, your practice will be concerned with God himself within you. For this is the end of all spiritual exercises - to turn the mind to the Lord God and rest in him with a completely pure understanding and a completely devoted will, without the entanglements and fantasies of the imagination. This sort of exercise is not practised by fleshly organs nor by the exterior senses, but by that by which one is indeed a man. For a man is precisely understanding and will. For that reason, in so far as a man is still playing with the products of the imagination and the senses, and holds to them, it is obvious that he has not yet emerged from the motivation and limitations of his animal nature, that is of that which he shares in common with the animals. For these know and feel objects by means of recognised shapes and sense impressions and no more, since they do not possess the higher powers of the soul. But it is different with man, who is created in the image and likeness of God with understanding, will, and free choice, through which he should be directly, purely and nakedly impressed and united with God, and firmly adhere to him. For this reason the Devil tries eagerly and with all his power to hinder this practice so far as he can, being envious of this in man, since it is a sort of prelude and initiation of eternal life. So he is always trying to draw man's mind away from the Lord God, now by temptations or passions, now by superfluous worries and pointless cares, now by restlessness and distracting conversation and senseless curiosity, now by the study of subtle books, irrelevant discussion, gossip and news, now by hardships, now by opposition, etc. Such matters may seem trivial enough and hardly sinful, but they are a great hindrance to this holy exercise and practice. Therefore, even if they may appear useful and necessary, they should be rejected, whether great or small, as harmful and dangerous, and put out of our minds. Above all therefore it is necessary that things heard, seen, done and said, and other such things, must be received without adding things from the imagination, without mental associations and without emotional involvement, and one should not let past or future associations, implications or constructs of the imagination form and grow. For when constructs of the imagination are not allowed to enter the memory and mind, a man is not hindered, whether he be engaged in prayer, meditation, or reciting psalms, or in any other practice or spiritual exercise, nor will they recur again. So commit yourself confidently and without hesitation, all that you are, and everything else, individually and in general, to the unfailing and totally reliable providence of God, in silence and in peace, and he will fight for you. He will liberate you and comfort you more fully, more effectively and more satisfactorily than if you were to dream about it all the time, day and night, and were to cast around frantically all over the place with the futile and confused thoughts of your mind in bondage, nor will you wear out your mind and body, wasting your time, and stupidly and pointlessly exhausting your strength. So accept everything, separately and in general, wherever it comes from and whatever its origin, in silence and peace, and with an equal mind, as coming to you from a father's hand and his divine providence. So render your imagination bare of the images of all physical things as is appropriate to your state and profession, so that you can cling to him with a bare and undivided mind, as you have so often and so completely vowed to do, without anything whatever being able to come between your soul and him, so that you can pass purely and unwaveringly from the wounds of his humanity into the light of his divinity.

CHAPTER 5

On purity of heart which is to be sought above all things

If your desire and aim is to reach the destination of the path and home of true happiness, of grace and glory, by a straight and safe way then earnestly apply your mind to seek constant purity of heart, clarity of mind and calm of the senses. Gather up your heart's desire and fix it continually on the Lord God above. To do so you must withdraw yourself so far as you can from friends and from everyone else, and from the activities that hinder you from such a purpose. Grasp every opportunity when you can find the place, time and means to devote yourself to silence and contemplation, and gathering the secret fruits of silence, so that you can escape the shipwreck of this present age and avoid the restless agitation of the noisy world. For this reason apply yourself at all times to purity, clarity and peace of heart above all things, so that, so far as possible, you can keep the doors of your heart resolutely barred to the forms and images of the physical senses and worldly imaginations by shutting off the doors of the physical senses and turning within yourself. After all, purity of heart is recognised as the most important thing among all spiritual practices, as its final aim, and the reward for all the labours that a spiritual-minded person and true religious may undertake in this life. For this reason you should with all care, intelligence and effort free your heart, senses and desires from everything that can hinder their liberty, and above all from everything in the world that could possibly bind and overcome you. So struggle in this way to draw together all the distractions of your heart and desires of your mind into one true, simple and supreme good, to keep them gathered within yourself in one place, and by this means to remain always joined to things divine and to God in your mind, to abandon the unreliable things of earth, and be able to translate your mind continually to the things above within yourself in Jesus Christ. To which end, if you have begun to strip and purify yourself of images and imaginations and to simplify and still your heart and mind in the Lord God so that you can draw and taste the well of divine grace in everything within yourself, and so that you are united to God in your mind by a good will, then this itself is enough for you in place of all study and reading of holy scripture, and as demonstration of love of God and neighbour, as devotion itself testifies. So simplify your heart with all care, diligence and effort so that still and at peace from the products of the imagination you can turn round and remain always in the Lord within yourself, as if your mind were already in the now of eternity, that is of the godhead. In this way you will be able to renounce yourself through love of Jesus Christ, with a pure heart, clean conscience and unfeigned faith, and commit yourself completely and fully to God in all difficulties and eventualities, and be willing to submit yourself patiently to his will and good pleasure at all times. For this to come about you must repeatedly retreat into your heart and remain there, keeping yourself free from everything, so far as is possible. You must always keep the eye of your mind clear and still. You must guard your understanding from daydreams and thoughts of earthly things. You must completely free the inclination of your will from worldly cares and cling with all your being to the supreme true good with fervent love. You must keep your memory always lifted up and firmly anchored in that same true supreme good and only uncreated reality. In just this way your whole mind gathered up with all its powers and faculties in God, may become one spirit with him, in whom the supreme perfection of life is known to consist. This is the true union of spirit and love by which a man is made compliant to all the impulses of the supreme and eternal will, so that he becomes by grace what God is by nature. At the same time it should be noted that in the very moment in which one is able, by God's help, to overcome one's own will, that is to cast away from oneself inordinate love or strong feeling, in other words so as to dare simply to trust God completely in all one's needs, by this very fact one becomes so pleasing to God that his grace is imparted to one, and through that very grace one experiences that true love and devotion which drives out all uncertainty and fear and has full confidence in God. What is more, there can be no greater happiness than to place one's all in him who lacks nothing. So why do you still remain in yourself where you cannot stay. Cast yourself, all of yourself, with confidence into God and he will sustain you, heal you and make you safe. If you dwell on these things faithfully within, they will do more to confer a happy life on you than all riches, pleasures and honours, and above all the wisdom and knowledge of this present deceitful world and its life, even if you were to excel in them all that ever lived.

CHAPTER 6

That the devout man should cleave to God with naked understanding and will

The more you strip yourself of the products of the imagination and involvement in external, worldly things and the objects of the senses, the more your soul will recover its strength and its inner senses so that it can appreciate the things which are above. So learn to withdraw from imaginations and the images of physical things, since what pleases God above everything is a mind bare of those sorts of forms and objects, for it is his delight to be with the sons of men, that is those who, at peace from such activities, distractions and passions, seek him with a pure and simple mind, empty themselves for him, and cleave to him. Otherwise, if your memory, imagination and thought is often involved with such things, you must needs be filled with the thought of new things or memories of old ones, or identified with other changing objects. As a result, the Holy Spirit withholds itself from thoughts bereft of understanding. So the true lover of Jesus Christ should be so united through good will in his understanding with the divine will and goodness, and be so bare of all imaginations and passions that he does not even notice whether he is being mocked or loved, or something is being done to him. For a good will turns everything to good and is above everything. So if the will is good and is obedient and united to God with pure understanding, he is not hurt even if the flesh and the senses and the outer man is moved to evil, and is slow to good, or even if the inner man is slow to feel devotion, but should simply cleave to God with faith and good will in naked understanding. He is doing this if he is conscious of all his own imperfection and nothingness, recognises his good to consist in his Creator alone, abandons himself with all his faculties and powers, and all creatures, and immerses himself wholly and completely in the Creator, so that he directs all his actions purely and entirely in his Lord God, and seeks nothing apart from him, in whom he recognises all good and all joy of perfection to be found. And he is so transformed in a certain sense into God that he cannot think, understand, love or remember anything but God himself and the things of God. Other creatures however and even himself he does not see, except in God, nor does he love anything except God alone, nor remember anything about them or himself except in God. This knowledge of the truth always makes the soul humble, ready to judge itself and not others, while on the contrary worldly wisdom makes the soul proud, futile, inflated and puffed up with wind. So let this be the fundamental spiritual doctrine leading to the knowledge of God, his service and familiarity with him, that if you want to truly possess God, you must strip your heart of all love of things of the senses, not just of certain creatures, so that you can turn to the Lord your God with a simple and whole heart and with all your power, freely and without any double-mindedness, care or anxiety, but with full confidence in his providence alone about everything.

CHAPTER 7

How the heart should be gathered within itself

What is more, as is said in the book On the Spirit and the Soul (of St. Augustine), to ascend to God means to enter into oneself. He who entering within and penetrating his inmost nature, goes beyond himself, he is truly ascending to God. So let us withdraw our hearts from the distractions of this world, and recall them to the inner joys, so that we can establish them to some degree in the light of divine contemplation. For this is the life and peace of our hearts - to be established by intent in the love of God, and to be sweetly remade by his comforting. But the reason why we are in so many ways hindered in the practical enjoyment of this matter and are unable to get into it is clearly because the human mind is so distracted by worries that it cannot bring its memory to turn within, is so clouded by its imaginations that it cannot return to itself with its understanding, and is so drawn away by its desires that it is quite unable to come back to itself by desire for inner sweetness and spiritual joy. Thus it is so prostrate among the sense objects presented to it that it cannot enter into itself as the image of God. It is therefore right and necessary for the mind to raise itself above itself and everything created by the abandonment of everything, with humble reverence and great trust, and to say within itself, He whom I seek, love, thirst for and desire from everything and more than anything is not a thing of the senses or the imagination, but is above everything that can be experienced by the senses and the intellect. He cannot be experienced by any of the senses, but is completely desirable to my will. He is moreover not discernable, but is perfectly desirable to my inner affections. He cannot be comprehended, but can be loved in his fullness with a pure heart, for he is above all lovable and desirable, and of infinite goodness and perfection. And then a darkness comes over the mind and it is raised up into itself and penetrates even deeper. And the more inward-looking the desire for it, the more powerful this means of ascent to the mysterious contemplation of the holy Trinity in Unity and Unity in Trinity in Jesus Christ is, and the more interior the yearning, the more productive it is. Certainly in matters spiritual the more inward they are the greater they are as spiritual experiences. For this reason, never give up, never stop until you have tasted some pledge, as I might say, or foretaste of the future full experience, and until you have obtained the satisfaction of however small a first fruits of the divine joy. And do not give up pursuing it and following its scent until you have seen the God of gods in Sion. Do not stop or turn back in your spiritual journey and your union and adherence to God within you until you have achieved what you have been seeking. Take as a pattern of this the example of those climbing an ordinary mountain. If our mind is involved by its desires in the things which are going on below, it is immediately carried away by endless distractions and side tracks, and being to some extent divided against itself, is weakened and as it were scattered amongst the things which it seeks with its desires. The result is ceaseless movement, travel without an arrival, and labour without rest. If on the other hand our heart and mind can withdraw itself by its desire and love from the infinite distraction below of the things beneath it, can learn to be with itself, abandoning these lower things and gathering itself within itself into the one unchanging and satisfying good, and can hold to it inseparably with its will, it is correspondingly more and more gathered together in one and strengthened, as it is raised up by knowledge and desire. In this way it will become accustomed to the true supreme good within itself until it will be made completely immovable and arrive securely at that true life which is the Lord God himself, so that it can now rest in him within and in peace without any changeability or vicissitude of time, perfectly gathered within itself in the secret divine abode in Christ Jesus who is the way for those who come to him, the truth and life.

CHAPTER 8

How a religious man should commit himself to God in all circumstances whatsoever

I am now completely convinced that you will recognise from these arguments that the more you strip yourself of the products of your imagination and all worldly and created things, and are united to God with your intellect by a good will, the closer you will approach the state of innocence and perfection. What could be better? And what could be more happy and joyful? Above all it is important for you to keep your mind bare - without imaginations and images and free of any sort of entanglement, so that you are not concerned about either the world, friends, prosperity or adversity, or anything present, past or future, whether in yourself or in others - not even your own sins. But consider yourself with a certain pure simplicity to be alone with God outside the world, and as if your mind were already in eternity and separated from the body so that it will certainly not bother about worldly things or be concerned about the state of the world, about peace or war, about good weather or rain, or about anything at all in this world, but with complete docility will turn to God alone, be empty for him and cleave to him. So now in this way ignore your body and all created things, present or future, and direct the high point of your mind and spirit directly, as best you can, naked and unencumbered on the uncreated light. And let your spirit be cleansed in this way from all imaginations, coverings and things obscuring its vision, like an angel (not) tied to a body, who is not hindered by the works of the flesh nor tangled in vain and wandering thoughts. Let your spirit therefore arm itself against all temptations, vexations, and injuries so that it can persevere steadily in God when attacked by either face of fortune. So that when some inner disturbance or boredom or mental confusion come you will not be indignant or dejected because of it, nor run back to vocal prayers or other forms of consolation, but only to lift yourself up in your intellect by a good will to hold on to God with your mind whether the natural inclination of the body wills it or not. The religious-minded soul should be so united to God and should have or render its will so conformed to the divine will that it is not occupied with any created thing or cling to it any more than before it was created, and as if nothing existed except God and the soul itself. And in this way it should accept everything confidently and equally, in general and in particular, from the hand of divine providence, agreeing in everything with the Lord in patience, peace and silence. The thing is that the most important thing of all for a spiritual life is to strip the mind of all imaginations so that one can be united in one's intellect to God by a good will, and conformed to him. Besides, nothing will then be intermediary between you and God. This is obvious, since nothing external will stand between you when by the vow of voluntary poverty you will have removed the possession of anything whatsoever, and by the vow of chastity you will have abandoned your body, and by obedience you will have given up your will and your soul itself. And in this way nothing will be left to stand between you and God. That you are a religious person is indicated by your profession, your state, and now your habit and tonsure and such like, but whether you are only a religious in appearance or a real one, you will find out. Bear in mind therefore how greatly you have fallen away and sin against the Lord your God and all his justice if you behave otherwise and cling with your will and love to what is created rather than to the Creator himself, putting the created before the Creator.

CHAPTER 9

How much the contemplation of God is to be preferred to all other exercises

Now since all things other than God are the effect and work of the Creator himself, their having ability and being is a limited power and existence, and being as they are created out of nothing, they are circumscribed by the effects of their nothingness, while their tendency of themselves towards nothingness means that we receive our existence, preservation and activity moment by moment from the Creator himself, along with whatever other qualities created things may have, just as we receive their insufficiency to any action of themselves, both with regard to themselves and to others, in relation to him whose operation they are, they remain as a nothing before something which exists, and as something finite before what is infinite. For this reason let all our actual contemplation, life and activity take place in him alone, about him, for him and towards him who is able and capable to produce with a single nod of his will things infinitely more perfect than any that exist now. No contemplation and fruition of love, whether intellectual or affective, is more useful, more perfect and more satisfying than that which is of God himself, the Creator, our supreme and true Good, from whom, through whom and to whom are all things. He is infinitely satisfying both to himself and to all others, who contains within himself in absolute simplicity and from all eternity the perfection of all things, in whom there is nothing which is not himself, before whom and through whom remain the causes of all things impermanent, and in whom dwell the unchanging origins of all changing things, while even the eternal reasons of all temporal things, rational and irrational, abide in him. He brings everything to completion, and fills all things, in general and in particular, completely and essentially with himself. He is more intimately and more really present to everything by his being than each thing is to itself, for in him all things are united together, and live in him eternally. What is more, if someone, out of weakness or from lack of intellectual practice, is detained longer in the contemplation of created things, this supreme, true and fruitful contemplation may still be seen as possible for mortal man, so that there may take place an upward leap in all his contemplations and meditations, whether about created things or the Creator, and the appreciation of God the Creator himself, the One and

Three, may surge up within so that he come to burn with the fire of divine love and the true life in himself and in others, in such a way as to make him deserving of the joy of eternal life. Even in this one should bear in mind the difference between the contemplation of faithful Catholics and that of pagan philosophers, for the contemplation of the philosophers is for the perfection of the contemplator himself, and consequently it is confined to the intellect and their aim in it is intellectual knowledge. But the contemplation of the Saints, and of Catholics, is for the love of him, that is of the God they are contemplating. As a result it is not confined in the final analysis to the intellect in knowledge, but crosses over into the will through love. That is why the Saints in their contemplation have the love of God as their principal aim, since it is more satisfying to know and possess even the Lord Jesus Christ spiritually through grace than physically or even really but without grace. Furthermore, while the soul is withdrawn from everything and is turned within, the eye of contemplation is opened and sets itself up a ladder by which it can pass to the contemplation of God. By this contemplation the soul is set on fire for eternal things by the heavenly and divine good things it experiences, and views all the things of time from a distance and as if they were nothing. Hence when we approach God by the way of negation, we first deny him everything that

ON CLEAVING TO GOD

can be experienced by the body, the senses and the imagination, secondly even things experienceable by the intellect, and finally even being itself in so far as it is found in created things. This, so far as the nature of the way is concerned, is the best means of union with God, according to Dionysius. And this is the cloud in which God is said to dwell, which Moses entered, and through this came to the inaccessible light. Certainly, it is not the spiritual which comes first, but the natural, (1 Corinthians 15.46) so one must proceed by the usual order of things, from active work to the quiet of contemplation, and from moral virtues to spiritual and contemplative realities. Finally, my soul, why are you uselessly preoccupied with so many things, and always busy with them? Seek out and love the one supreme good, in which is all that is worth seeking, and that will be enough for you. Unhappy therefore is he who knows and possesses everything other than this, and does not know this. While if he knows everything as well as this, it is not from knowing them that he is better off but because of This. That is why John says, This is eternal life, to know Thee, etc. (John 17.3) and the prophet says, I will be satisfied when your glory becomes manifest. (Psalm 17.15)

CHAPTER 10

That one should not be concerned about feeling tangible devotion so much as about cleaving to God with one's will

Furthermore you should not be much concerned about tangible devotion, the experience of sweetness or tears, but rather that you should be mentally united with God within yourself by a good will in your intellect. For what pleases God above everything is a mind free from imaginations, that is images, ideas and the representations of created things. It befits a monk to be indifferent to everything created so that he can turn easily and barely to God alone within himself, be empty for him and cleave to him. For this reason deny yourself so that you can follow Christ, the Lord your God, in nakedness, who was himself poor, obedient, chaste, humble and suffering, and in whose life and death many were scandalised, as is clear from the Gospel accounts. After all, a soul which is separated from the body pays no attention to what is done to its abandoned body - whether it is burned, hanged, or reviled, and is in no way saddened by the afflictions imposed on the body, but thinks only of the Now of eternity and the One Thing which the Lord calls necessary in the Gospel. So you too should treat your body as if you were no longer in the body, but think always of the eternity of your soul in God, and direct your thoughts carefully to that One Thing of which Christ said, For one thing is necessary. (Luke 10.42) You will experience because of it great grace, helping you towards the acquisition of nakedness of mind and simplicity of heart. Indeed this One Thing is very much present with you if you have made yourself bare of imaginations and all other entanglements, and you will soon experience that this is so - namely when you can be empty and cleave to God with a naked and resolute mind. In this way you will remain unconquered in whatever may be inflicted on you, like the holy martyrs, fathers, the elect, and indeed all the saints who despised everything and only thought of their souls' security and eternity in God. Armed in this way within, and united to God through a good will, they spurned everything of the world as if their souls were already separated from their bodies. Consider from this how much a good will united with God is capable of, when by means of its pressing towards God the soul is effectively separated from the body in spirit and looks on its outward man as it were from a distance, and as not belonging to it. In this way it despises everything that is inflicted on itself or on its flesh as if they were happening to someone else, or not to a human being at all. For He that is united with the Lord is one Spirit, (1 Corinthians 6.17) that is with him. So you should never dare to think or imagine anything before the Lord your God that you would blush to be heard or seen in before men, since your respect for God should be even greater than for them. It is a matter of justice in fact that all your thoughts and thinking should be raised to God alone, and the highest point of your mind should only be directed to him as if nothing existed but him, and holding to him may enjoy the perfect beginning of the life to come.

CHAPTER 11

How one should resist temptations and bear trials

Now there is no one who approaches God
with a true and upright heart who is not tested by
hardships and temptations. So in all these temptations see to it that even if you feel them, you do
not consent to them, but bear them patiently and
calmly with humility and long suffering. Even if
they are blasphemies and sordid, hold firmly on to
this fact in everything, that you can do nothing
better or more effective against them than to consider all this sort of fantasy as a nothing. Even if
they are the most vile, sordid and horrible blasphemies, simply take no notice of them, count
them as nothing and despise them. Don't look on
them as yours or allow yourself to make them a
matter of conscience. The enemy will certainly
take flight if you treat him and his company with
contempt in this way. He is very proud and cannot
bear to be despised and spurned. So the best rem-
edy is to completely ignore all such temptations,
like flies flying around in front of your eyes

against your will. The servant of Jesus Christ must see to it that he is not so easily forced to withdraw from the face of the Lord and to be annoyed, murmur and complain over the nuisance of a single fly, that is, a trivial temptation, suspicion, sadness, distraction, need or any such adversity, when they can all be put to flight with no more than the hand of a good will directed up to God. After all, through a good will a man has God as his defender, and the holy angels as his guardians and protectors. What is more, any temptation can be overcome by a good will too, like a fly driven away from a bald head by one's hand. So peace is for men of good will. Indeed we can offer God nothing more valuable than a good will, since a good will in the soul is the source of all good things, and the mother of all virtues. If any one is beginning to possess that good will, he undoubtedly has what is necessary for leading a good life. For if you want what is good, but cannot do it, God will make good the deed. For it is in accordance with this eternal law that God has established with irrevocable firmness that deserts should be a matter of the will, whether in bliss or torment, reward or punishment. Love itself is a great will to serve God, a sweet desire to please God, and a fervent wish to experience God. What is more, to be tempted is not a sin, but the opportunity for exercising virtue, so that temptation can be greatly to a man's benefit, since it is held that the whole of a man's life on earth is a testing. (Job 7.1)

CHAPTER 12

How powerful the love of God is

All that is said above and whatever is necessary for salvation cannot be better, more immediately and more securely achieved than by love, through which whatever is lacking of what is necessary for salvation can be made good. In love we possess the fullness of all good and the realisation of our highest longing is not denied us. After all it is love alone by which we turn back to God, are changed into God, cleave to God, and are united to God in such a way that we become one spirit with him, and are by him and through him made blessed here by grace and hereafter in glory. Now love is such that it cannot rest except in the beloved, but it does when it wins the beloved in full and peaceful possession. For love, which itself is charity, is the way of God to men and the way of man to God. God cannot house where there is no love. So if we have love, we have God, for God is love. Furthermore nothing is sharper than love, nothing is more subtle, nothing more penetrating.

It will not rest until it has by its very nature penetrated the whole power, the depth and the totality of the loved one. It wants to make itself one with the beloved, and itself, if it were possible, to be what the beloved is too. Thus it cannot bear that anything should stand between itself and the beloved object, which is God, but presses eagerly towards him. As a result it never rests until it has left everything else behind and come to him alone. For the nature of love is of a unitive and transforming power which transforms the lover into what he loves, or alternatively, makes the lover one with the other, and vice versa, in so far as is possible. This is manifest in the first place with regard to the mental powers, depending on how much the beloved is in the lover, in other words depending on how sweetly and delightfully the beloved is recalled in the mind of the lover, and in direct proportion, that is, with how much the lover strives to grasp all the things that relate to the beloved not just superficially but intimately, and to enter, as it were, into his innermost secrets. It is also manifest with regard to the emotional and affective powers when the beloved is said to be in the lover, in other words when the desire to please the beloved is found in the will and established within by the happy enjoyment of him. Alternatively, the lover is in the beloved when he is united with him by all his desire and compliance in agreement with the beloved's willing and not willing, and finds his own pleasure and pain in that of the beloved. For love draws the lover out of himself (since love is strong as death), and establishes him in the beloved, causing him to cleave closely to him. For the soul is more where it loves than where it lives, since it is in what it loves in accordance with its very nature, understanding and will, while it is in where it lives only with regard to form, which is even true for animals as well. There is nothing therefore which draws us away from the exterior senses to within ourselves, and from there to Jesus Christ and things divine, more than the love of Christ and the desire for the sweetness of Christ, for the experience, awareness and enjoyment of the presence of Christ's divinity. For there is nothing but the power of love which can lead the soul from the things of earth to the lofty summit of heaven. Nor can anyone attain the supreme beatitude unless summoned to it by love and yearning. Love after all is the life of the soul, the wedding garment and the soul's perfection, containing all the law and the prophets and our Lord's teaching. That is why Paul says to the Romans, Love is the fulfilling of the law, (Rom. 13.8) and in the first letter to Timothy, The end of the commandment is love. (1 Timothy 1.5)

CHAPTER 13

The nature and value of prayer, and how the heart should be recollected within itself

Besides this, since we are incapable of ourselves for this and for any other good action whatsoever, and since we can of ourselves offer nothing to the Lord God (from whom all good things come) which is not his already, with this one exception, as he has deigned to show us both by his own blessed mouth as well as by his example, that we should turn to him in all circumstances and occasions as guilty, wretched, poor, beggarly, weak, helpless, subject servants and sons. And that we should beseech him and lay before him with complete confidence the dangers that are besetting us on all sides, completely grief-stricken in ourselves, in humble prostration of mind, in fear and love, and with recollected, composed, mature, true and naked, shamefaced affection, with great yearning and determination, and in groaning of heart and sincerity of mind. Thus we commit and offer ourselves up to him freely, securely and nakedly, fully and in everything that is ours, holding nothing back to ourselves, in such a complete and final way, that the same is fulfilled in us as in our blessed father Isaac, who speaks of this very type of prayer, saying, Then we shall be one in God, and the Lord God will be all in all and alone in us when his own perfect love, with which he first loved us, will have become the disposition of our own hearts too. This will come about when all our love, all our desire, all our concern, all our efforts, in fact everything we think, everything we see, speak and even hope will be God, and that unity which now is of the Father with the Son, and of the Son with the Father, will be poured into our own heart and mind as well, in such a way that just as he loves us with sincere and indissoluble love we too will be joined to him with eternal and inseparable affection. In other words we shall be united with him in such a way that whatever we hope, and whatever we say or pray will be God. This therefore should be the aim, this the concern and goal of a spiritual man - to be worthy to possess the image of future bliss in this corruptible body, and in a certain measure experience in advance how the foretaste of that heavenly bliss, eternal life and glory begins in this world. This, as I say, is the goal of all perfection, that his purified mind should be daily raised up from all bodily objects to spiritual things until all his mental activity and all his heart's desire become one unbroken prayer. So the mind must abandon the dregs of earth and press on towards to God, on whom alone should be fixed the desire of a spiritual man, for whom the least separation from that summum bonum is to be considered a living death and dreadful loss. Then, when the requisite peace has been established in his mind, when it is free from attachment to any carnal passion, and clings firmly in intention to that one supreme good, the Apostle's sayings are fulfilled, Pray without ceasing, (1 Thessalonians 5.17) and, Pray in every place lifting up pure hands without anger or dispute. (1 Timothy 2.8) For when the power of the mind is absorbed in this purity, so to speak, and is transformed from an earthly nature into the spiritual or angelic likeness, whatever it receives into itself, whatever it is occupied with, whatever it is doing, it will be pure and sincere prayer. In this way, if you continue all the time in the way we have described from the beginning, it will become as easy and clear for you to remain in contemplation in your inward and recollected state, as to live in the natural state.

CHAPTER 14

That we should seek the verdict of our conscience in every decision

While we should strive for spiritual perfection of mind, purity and peace in God, it will be found to be not a little beneficial to this that we should return quietly into the inner secret place of the mind in the face of everything said, thought or done to us. There, withdrawn from everything else and completely recollected within ourselves, we can place ourselves in the knowledge of the truth before us and undoubtedly discover and understand that it does us absolutely no good, and rather the contrary, when we are praised or honoured by others while we recognise by the knowledge of the truth about ourselves within that we are blameworthy and guilty. And just as nothing is any help if externally people praise someone if his conscience internally accuses him, in the same way on the contrary it does a man no harm to be despised, maligned and persecuted when he remains internally just as innocent, blameless and without fault. On the contrary he has all the more good reason to rejoice in the Lord with patience, in peace and silence. After all no adversity can do any harm where evil is not in control, and just as no evil goes unpunished, so no good goes unrewarded. Nor should we wish a reward with hypocrites or expect and receive profit from men, but from the Lord God alone, not in the present, but in the future, and not in fleeting time, but in eternity. It is clear therefore that nothing is greater, and nothing better than to enter into the inner secret place of the mind always and in every tribulation and occurrence, and there to call upon the Lord Jesus Christ himself, our helper in temptations and tribulations, and to humble ourselves there by confession of sin, and praise God and Father himself, the giver of correction and the giver of consolation. Above all one should accept everything, in general and individually, in oneself or in others, agreeable or disagreeable, with a prompt and confident spirit, as coming from the hand of his infallible Providence or the order he has arranged. This attitude will lead to the forgiveness of our sins, the deliverance from bitterness, the enjoyment of joy and security, the outpouring of grace and mercy, introduction and establishment into a close relationship with God, abundant enjoyment of his presence, and firm cleaving and union with him. But let us not copy those who from hypocrisy and Pharisaism want to appear better and different from what they are, and to make a better impression and appearance before men of being something special, than they know in truth inside to be so. For it is absolute madness to seek, hunger for and aspire to human praise or renown, from oneself or others, when one is in spite of it all inwardly full of cravings and serious faults. And certainly the good things we have talked about above will flee him who chases such vanities, and he will merely bring disgrace on himself. So always keep your faults and your own incapacity before your eyes, and know yourself, so that you can be humbled and not try to avoid being held as the lowest, vilest and most abject scum by everyone when you are aware of the grave sins and serious faults in yourself. For which reason consider yourself compared to others as dross to gold, weeds to the wheat, chaff to the grain, a wolf to the sheep, Satan to the children of God. And do not seek to be respected by others and given precedence before others, but rather flee with all your heart and soul the poison of this disease, the venom of praise, the concern for boasting and vanity, lest, as the prophet says, The wicked is praised in his own heart's desires, (Psalm 10.4) and Isaiah, They who speak good of you, deceive you and destroy the way of your feet, (Isaiah 3.12) and the Lord in Luke, Woe to you when men speak well of you! (Luke 6.26).

CHAPTER 15

How contempt of himself can be produced in a man, and how useful it is

Furthermore the more a man recognises his own insignificance, the more he fully and the more clearly he becomes aware to the divine majesty, and the more a man is low in his own eyes for the sake of God, the truth and justice, the more precious he is in the eyes of God. For this reason let us strive with the whole strength of our desire to consider ourselves the lowest of all and to consider ourselves unworthy of any favour. We should strive to be displeasing to ourselves and pleasing only to God, while regarded as low and unworthy of consideration by others. Above all not to be moved by difficulties, afflictions and insults, and not to be upset by those who inflict such things on us, or entertain evil thoughts against them or be indignant, but to believe steadfastly and with equanimity in all insults, slights, blows and dereliction that it is only appropriate. For in truth he who is really penitent and grieving before

God hates to be honoured and loved by all, and does not try to manipulate things so as to avoid being to some degree hated, neglected and despised right to the end, so that he can be truly humbled and sincerely cleave to God alone with a pure heart. Indeed, for loving God alone and hating oneself more than anything, and desiring to be despised by others we do not require external work or physical strength, but rather physical solitude, the labour of the heart, and peace of mind so that, as it were, by labour of the heart and the disposition of the inmost mind, one may rise up, casting off from oneself lower and physical things, and so soar up, ascending to things heavenly and divine. For indeed in so doing we are changed into God, and this will especially take place when without judgement, condemnation or contempt of our neighbour, we choose rather to be considered as scum and a disgrace by everyone and to be despised as unclean filth by everyone than to experience all sorts of different delicacies or to be honoured and exalted by men, or enjoy all sorts of transitory physical forms of well-being and comfort. We should not desire any pleasure of this present, mortal and physical life but rather to mourn, bewail and lament our offences, faults and sins without ceasing, and to perfectly despise and annihilate ourselves, and from day to day to be considered more and more abject by others, while in all our insignificance we become worthless even in our own eyes, so that we can be pleasing to God alone, love him alone, and cleave to him alone. We should not wish to be concerned about anything except the Lord Jesus Christ himself who alone should reside in our affections, and we should not be concerned or anxious about anything except him on whose dominion and providence everything in general and individually depends. So from now on it should not be your aim to seek enjoyment but to truly mourn with all your heart. For that reason, if you do not mourn, mourn for that, while if you do mourn, mourn especially that you have brought the cause of your pain on yourself by your own great offences and infinite sins. For just as a condemned man on receiving his sentence does not concern himself about the seating of the spectators, so he who laments and is genuinely mourning is not interested in pleasures, resentment, fame or wrongs or things of that sort. And just as townsfolk and contemned criminals have different accommodation, the state and position of those who are mourning and have committed offences deserving punishment ought to be completely different from those who are innocent and under no obligation. Otherwise there would be no difference between the guilty and the innocent in matters of punishment and reward. The result would be great dereliction of duty, and evil behaviour would have more freedom than goodness. So everything must be renounced, everything despised, everything rejected and avoided, so that we can lay a firm foundation of penitent grieving. Then, loving Jesus Christ in reality, yearning for him, and holding him in one's heart, in reality experiencing pain for one's sins and faults, in reality seeking to know the coming Kingdom, while with true faith bearing in mind the reality of the torments and eternal judgement, and firmly and fully taking up the recollection and fear of one's own death, we should be aware of nothing else, and not care or be worried about anything else. For that reason, he who hurries towards the blessed state of impassibility and towards God should reckon himself to have experienced great loss every day that he is not insulted and despised. Impassibility after all is freedom from vices and passions and purity of heart and the adornment of all virtues. So consider yourself as already dead since there is no doubt that you have got to die. And as a final thought let this be the test for you of whether any thought, word or action of yours is of God, whether you are made more humble because of it, more inward and more recollected and established in God. If you find it is otherwise in yourself, you should be suspicious about it, whether it be not according to God, unacceptable to you and not to your benefit.

CHAPTER 16

How God's Providence includes everything

Certainly if we are to come directly, safely and nakedly to our Lord God without hindrance, freely and peacefully, as explained above, and be securely joined to him with even mind in prosperity or adversity, whether in life or in death, then our job is to commit everything unhesitatingly and resolutely, in general and individually, to his unquestionable and infallible providence. This is hardly surprising since it is he alone who gives to all things their being, their capacity and their action - that is, their strength, operation, nature, manner and order in number, weight and measure. Especially since just as a work of art presupposes a prior operation of nature, in the same way the operation of nature presupposes the work of God, creating, sustaining, ordering and administering it, for to him alone belong infinite power, wisdom, goodness and inherent mercy, justice, truth, love, and unchanging timelessness and omnipresence. So nothing can exist or act by its own power unless it acts in the power of God himself, who is the prime mover and the first principle, who is the cause of every action, and the actor in every agent. For so far as the nature of the order of things is concerned, God provides for everything without intermediary right down to the last detail. So nothing, from the greatest to the smallest things, can escape God's eternal providence, or fall away from it, whether in matters of the will, of causal events, or even of accidental circumstances outside of one's control. But God cannot do anything which does not fall under the order of his own providence, just as he cannot do anything which is not subject to its operation. Divine providence therefore extends to everything, in general and in particular, even including a man's thoughts. On which subject Scripture has this to say, Cast all your worries upon him, for he takes care of you. (1 Peter 5.7) And again the prophet says, Cast your care upon the Lord, and he will feed you. (Psalm 55.22) And, Look at the nations of men, my son, and see that no one ever put his trust in the Lord, and was disappointed. For who has been faithful to his commandments and been abandoned? (Sirach 2.22) And our Lord himself said, Do not be anxious, saying, What shall we eat? (Matthew 6.25) So whatever and however much we can hope from God, we shall undoubtedly receive, as Deuteronomy says, Every place where you feet tread shall be yours. (Deuteronomy

11.24) For a man shall receive all that he is able to desire, and so far as he can reach with his foot of faith, even so much shall he possess. That is why Bernard says, "God, the maker of everything is so abounding in mercy that whatever size grace cup of faith we are able to hold out to him, we shall undoubtedly have it filled." And so Mark has it, All that you ask in prayer believing that you will receive it, will be given you. (Mark 11.24) So the stronger and the more vehement our faith in God is, and the more reverently and persistently it is offered up to God, the more surely, the more abundantly and the quicker what we hoped for will be accomplished and obtained. Indeed if in doing this our faith in God is weak and slow to rise to God on account of the multitude and magnitude of our sins, we should remember this, that everything is possible with God, and that what he wishes is bound to take place, while what he does not wish cannot possibly happen, and that it is as easy for him to forgive and cancel countless sins, however enormous, as to do it with a single sin. While a sinner cannot, of himself, rise from innumerable sins, and free and absolve himself from them, and not even from just one sin. For we are unable not only to do, but even to think anything good, of ourselves, but this is from God. Nonetheless it is much more dangerous, other things being equal, to be ensnared in many sins than in a single one, since no sin is left unpunished, and every mortal sin deserves infinite punishment, and this by the rigour of justice since any such sin is against God who is indeed worthy of infinite reverence, dignity and honour. What is more, according to the Apostle Paul, God knows his own (2 Timothy 2.19), and it is impossible for any of them to perish by the whirlwinds and floods of any error, scandal, schism, persecution, heresy, tribulation, adversity or temptation, for he has foreseen from eternity and unchangeably the number of his elect and the extent of their merits in such a way that everything good and bad, what is theirs and not theirs, prosperity and adversity, all work together for them for good, except indeed that they appear even more glorious and commendable in adversity. So let us commit everything with full assurance, in general and in particular, confidently and unhesitatingly to divine providence, by which God permits however much and whatever sort of evil to happen to us. For it is good and will lead to good, since he permits it to exist, and it would not exist unless he permitted it to exist. Nor could it exist otherwise or more than he permits it to, because he knows how to, has the power to, and wills to change and convert it into something better. For just as it is by operation of providence that all good things exist, so it is by its permission that all bad things are changed into good. In this way in fact God's power, wisdom and mercy are shown forth through Christ our redeemer - his mercy and his justice, the power of grace and the weakness of nature, the beauty of everything in the association of opposites, the approval of the good, and the malice and punishment of the wicked. Similarly the contrition of the converted sinner, his confession, and penitence, the kindness of God, piety, charity and his praise and goodness (all show forth God's power and wisdom). Yet it does not always lead to good in those who do ill, but, as is usually the case, to great danger and extreme evil, in the loss, that is, of grace and their place in glory, and in the incurring of guilt and punishment, sometimes even eternal punishment, from which may Jesus Christ defend us. Amen.

You may also enjoy ...

Wandering Between Two Worlds: Essays on Faith and Art
Anita Mathias
Benediction Books, 2007
152 pages
ISBN: 0955373700

Available from www.amazon.com, www.amazon.co.uk
www.wanderingbetweentwoworlds.com

In these wide-ranging lyrical essays, Anita Mathias writes, in lush, lovely prose, of her naughty Catholic childhood in Jamshedpur, India; her large, eccentric family in Mangalore, a sea-coast town converted by the Portuguese in the sixteenth century; her rebellion and atheism as a teenager in her Himalayan boarding school, run by German missionary nuns, St. Mary's Convent, Nainital; and her abrupt religious conversion after which she entered Mother Teresa's convent in Calcutta as a novice. Later rich, elegant essays explore the dualities of her life as a writer, mother, and Christian in the United States-- Domesticity and Art, Writing and Prayer, and the experience of being "an alien and stranger" as an immigrant in America, sensing the need for roots.

About the Author

Anita Mathias was born in India, has a B.A. and M.A. in English from Somerville College, Oxford University and an M.A. in Creative Writing from the Ohio State University. Her essays have been published in The Washington Post, The London Magazine, The Virginia Quarterly Review, Commonweal, Notre Dame Magazine, America, The Christian Century, Religion Online, The Southwest Review, Contemporary Literary Criticism, New Letters, The Journal, and two of HarperSanFrancisco's The Best Spiritual Writing anthologies. Her non-fiction has won fellowships from The National Endowment for the Arts; The Minnesota State Arts Board; The Jerome Foundation, The Vermont Studio Center; The Virginia Centre for the Creative Arts, and the First Prize for the Best General Interest Article from the Catholic Press Association of the United States and Canada. Anita has taught Creative Writing at the College of William and Mary, and now lives and writes in Oxford, England.
Website: www.anitamathias.com/
Blog: wanderingbetweentwoworlds.blogspot.com/

.

Milton Keynes UK
Ingram Content Group UK Ltd.
UKHW011430301123
433560UK00004B/22

9 781849 028424